REVIEW COPY
COURTESY OF
ENSLOW PUBLISHERS, INC.

STATES

CONNECTICUT
A MyReportLinks.com Book

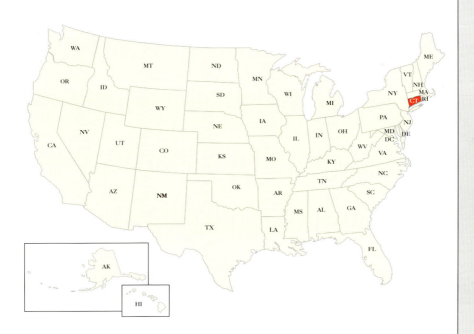

Ron Knapp

MyReportLinks.com Books
an imprint of
Enslow Publishers, Inc.
Box 398, 40 Industrial Road
Berkeley Heights, NJ 07922
USA

For Jan and Rick Albaugh

MyReportLinks.com Books, an imprint of Enslow Publishers, Inc. MyReportLinks is a trademark of Enslow Publishers, Inc.

Copyright © 2003 by Enslow Publishers, Inc.

All rights reserved.

No part of this book may be reproduced by any means without the written permission of the publisher.

Library of Congress Cataloging-in-Publication Data

Knapp, Ron.
  Connecticut / Ron Knapp.
    p. cm. — (States)
  Includes bibliographical references (p.) and index.
  Summary: Discusses the land and climate, economy, government, and history of Connecticut. Includes Internet links to Web sites related to Connecticut.
  ISBN 0-7660-5121-8
  1. Connecticut—Juvenile literature. [1. Connecticut.] I. Title. II. States (Series : Berkeley Heights, N.J.)
  F94.3 .K59 2003
  974.6—dc21
                          2002153555

Printed in the United States of America

10 9 8 7 6 5 4 3 2 1

To Our Readers:

Through the purchase of this book, you and your library gain access to the Report Links that specifically back up this book.

The Publisher will provide access to the Report Links that back up this book and will keep these Report Links up to date on **www.myreportlinks.com** for three years from the book's first publication date.

We have done our best to make sure all Internet addresses in this book were active and appropriate when we went to press. However, the author and the Publisher have no control over, and assume no liability for, the material available on those Internet sites or on other Web sites they may link to.

The usage of the MyReportLinks.com Books Web site is subject to the terms and conditions stated on the Usage Policy Statement on **www.myreportlinks.com**.

In the future, a password may be required to access the Report Links that back up this book. The password is found on the bottom of page 4 of this book.

Any comments or suggestions can be sent by e-mail to comments@myreportlinks.com or to the address on the back cover.

Photo Credits: © 2001, Robesus , Inc., p. 10; © Corel Corporation, p. 3; Connecticut Department of Environmental Protection, p. 18; Connecticut Historical Society, p. 25; Connecticut History Online, pp. 33, 43; Connecticut Office of Tourism, pp. 21, 45; Connecticut Women's Hall of Fame, p. 41; Dolan DNA Learning Center, p. 15; Enslow Publishers, Inc., pp. 1, 16; Goodyear Tire and Rubber Company, p. 13; Jim McElholm, Single Source Photography, p. 20; MyReportLinks.com Books, p. 4; Mystic Seaport, p. 22; National Archives and Records Administration, p. 27; Ringling Brothers and Barnum & Bailey Circus, p. 29; *The Hartford Courant*, p. 31; The Society of Colonial Wars in the State of Connecticut, pp. 35, 37, 39.

Cover Photo: Photo by Jim Steinhart of www.PlanetWare.com

Cover Description: Old State House, Hartford

Contents

	Report Links	4
	Connecticut Facts	10
1	**The State of Connecticut: Original Thinkers**	11
2	**Land and Climate**	16
3	**Famous Nutmeggers**	24
4	**Government and Economy**	32
5	**History**	35
	Chapter Notes	46
	Further Reading	47
	Index	48

About MyReportLinks.com Books

MyReportLinks.com Books
Great Books, Great Links, Great for Research!

MyReportLinks.com Books present the information you need to learn about your report subject. In addition, they show you where to go on the Internet for more information. The pre-evaluated Report Links that back up this book are kept up to date on **www.myreportlinks.com**. With the purchase of a MyReportLinks.com Books title, you and your library gain access to the Report Links that specifically back up that book. The Report Links save hours of research time and link to dozens—even hundreds—of Web sites, source documents, and photos related to your report topic.

Please see "To Our Readers" on the Copyright page for important information about this book, the MyReportLinks.com Books Web site, and the Report Links that back up this book.

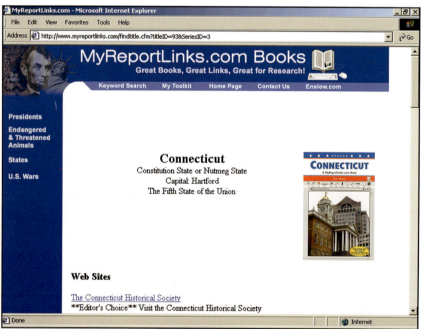

Access:

The Publisher will provide access to the Report Links that back up this book and will try to keep these Report Links up to date on our Web site for three years from the book's first publication date. Please enter **SCT7874** if asked for a password.

Tools   Search   Notes   Discuss

Report Links

 The Internet sites described below can be accessed at
http://www.myreportlinks.com

*Editor's choice

▶ The Connecticut Historical Society
At the Connecticut Historical Society Web site, you can view online exhibits that cover a variety of topics, search the library's vast collections, and learn about educational opportunities with the society.

Link to this Internet site from http://www.myreportlinks.com

*Editor's choice

▶ Connecticut's Gateway to History
The Connecticut's Gateway to History Web site investigates the state's past. Here you can explore online exhibits relating to Connecticut's government and find an online encyclopedia featuring brief biographies and descriptions of historical events.

Link to this Internet site from http://www.myreportlinks.com

*Editor's choice

▶ Connecticut History Online
Connecticut History Online explores the history of the Nutmeg State in text and photos.

Link to this Internet site from http://www.myreportlinks.com

*Editor's choice

▶ U.S. Census Bureau: Connecticut
The U.S. Census Bureau provides essential statistics about Connecticut, including facts about the state's population, demographics, businesses, geography, and more.

Link to this Internet site from http://www.myreportlinks.com

*Editor's choice

▶ Explore the States: Connecticut
America's Story from America's Library, a Library of Congress Web site, features interesting stories about Connecticut, such as the story of America's first hamburger, served in New Haven in 1895.

Link to this Internet site from http://www.myreportlinks.com

*Editor's choice

▶ World Almanac for Kids Online: Connecticut
World Almanac for Kids Online includes basic facts about Connecticut including population statistics, information about the government, economy, history, and much more.

Link to this Internet site from http://www.myreportlinks.com

Any comments? Contact us: comments@myreportlinks.com   5

Report Links

→ The Internet sites described below can be accessed at
http://www.myreportlinks.com

▶ **Barbara McClintock (1902–1992)**
The Dolan DNA Learning Center's Web site contains a biography of Connecticut native Barbara McClintock, a cytogeneticist who won the Nobel Prize in physiology or medicine in 1983 for her discovery of mobile genetic elements in plants.

Link to this Internet site from http://www.myreportlinks.com

▶ **Benedict Arnold's Leg**
Learn about Benedict Arnold, a native of Connecticut and famous Revolutionary War soldier who became an infamous traitor to his country.

Link to this Internet site from http://www.myreportlinks.com

▶ **Biographical Memoirs: Edwin Herbert Land**
This site offers an in-depth biography of Connecticut scientist Edwin Herbert Land, whose inventions led to "instant" film developing.

Link to this Internet site from http://www.myreportlinks.com

▶ **The City of New Haven Online**
Here you will learn about New Haven's history, government, economy, geography, parks, recreation, cultural attractions, and more.

Link to this Internet site from http://www.myreportlinks.com

▶ **Colonial Connecticut Records 1636–1776**
Facsimiles of the public records of the colony of Connecticut are offered in this site. Included are colonial charters, laws, letters, and court proceedings.

Link to this Internet site from http://www.myreportlinks.com

▶ **ConneCT—State of Connecticut**
Learn about Connecticut's state government, economy, history, symbols, geography, tourism, climate, and much more in this site. Click on "ConneCT Kids" for fun activities.

Link to this Internet site from http://www.myreportlinks.com

 Any comments? Contact us: **comments@myreportlinks.com**

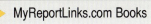

Tools   Search   Notes   Discuss   Go!

Report Links

 The Internet sites described below can be accessed at
http://www.myreportlinks.com

▶ Connecticut Freedom Trail
The Connecticut Freedom Trail Web site offers a tour of the historic sites that make up the Connecticut Freedom Trail, including stops on the Underground Railroad and places associated with the *Amistad* case.

Link to this Internet site from http://www.myreportlinks.com

▶ Connecticut's State Parks and Forests
Managed by Connecticut's Department of Environmental Protection, this site provides information on Connecticut's state parks and forests and includes maps, images, and directions.

Link to this Internet site from http://www.myreportlinks.com

▶ Connecticut Wildlife Division Kids Page
The Connecticut Department of Environmental Protection Web site includes a wide range of interesting activities for different age groups.

Link to this Internet site from http://www.myreportlinks.com

▶ Connecticut Wildlife Slide Shows
This Web site highlights the diverse wildlife that is to be found in Connecticut and includes a slide show of endangered and threatened species in the state.

Link to this Internet site from http://www.myreportlinks.com

▶ Connecticut Women's Hall of Fame
At the Connecticut Women's Hall of Fame Web site you can browse the Hall of Fame and read a biographical profile of each woman inducted.

Link to this Internet site from http://www.myreportlinks.com

▶ Everything You Ever Wanted to Know . . . About Connecticut
The Connecticut State Library brings together a variety of information about the state including genealogy, statistics, and facts about Connecticut's American Indians.

Link to this Internet site from http://www.myreportlinks.com

Any comments? Contact us: comments@myreportlinks.com

Report Links

The Internet sites described below can be accessed at
http://www.myreportlinks.com

▶ The Fundamental Orders
In 1639, three Connecticut towns made constitutional history by issuing the Fundamental Orders, the first written constitution in the Western Hemisphere. This site presents the original text of this historical document as well as a number of relevant links.

Link to this Internet site from http://www.myreportlinks.com

▶ Goodyear: Charles Goodyear and the Strange Story of Rubber
The Goodyear Tire and Rubber Company's Web site offers a biography of inventor Charles Goodyear and details of the "accident" which led to his discovery of the process of rubber vulcanization.

Link to this Internet site from http://www.myreportlinks.com

▶ Harriet Beecher Stowe Center: The Harriet Beecher Stowe House and Library
At the Harriet Beecher Stowe Center you will learn about the author's life, her connection to Connecticut, her neighbor Mark Twain, and much more.

Link to this Internet site from http://www.myreportlinks.com

▶ Hartford: New England's Rising Star
This Web site from the city of Hartford, Connecticut, contains information about the city's history, attractions, government, economy, neighborhoods, and much more.

Link to this Internet site from http://www.myreportlinks.com

▶ Mark Twain
Explore the life of Mark Twain through PBS Online's interactive scrapbook. Here you will learn about the time he spent in Connecticut and other interesting details about his life.

Link to this Internet site from http://www.myreportlinks.com

▶ Mashantucket Pequot Museum and Research Center
At the Mashantucket Pequot Museum and Research Center site you can take a virtual tour of the museum, learn about Pequot tribal history, search the library's archives, and find out about new exhibits and special events.

Link to this Internet site from http://www.myreportlinks.com

Any comments? Contact us: **comments@myreportlinks.com**

Tools Search Notes Discuss

 The Internet sites described below can be accessed at
http://www.myreportlinks.com

▶ Mystic Seaport
This Web site provides information about the ships and exhibits of the Mystic Seaport museum. Information about the landmarks of Mystic village can also be found here.

Link to this Internet site from http://www.myreportlinks.com

▶ Old State House—Hartford, Connecticut
The Old State House in Hartford, Connecticut, is the oldest state capitol still standing. This site provides a history of the State House as well as photos, comprehensive information for researchers and visitors, and activities for kids.

Link to this Internet site from http://www.myreportlinks.com

▶ Profiles in Connecticut Black History
Profiles in Connecticut Black History explores the lives and achievements of African Americans from Connecticut.

Link to this Internet site from http://www.myreportlinks.com

▶ Ringling Brothers and Barnum & Bailey: P. T. Barnum
The Web site of the Ringling Brothers and Barnum & Bailey Circus offers this biography of Phineas Taylor Barnum, master showman and native of Bethel, Connecticut.

Link to this Internet site from http://www.myreportlinks.com

▶ The Society of Colonial Wars in the State of Connecticut: Important Dates in Connecticut's History
Here you will find comprehensive articles about Adriaen Block, John Oldham, Thomas Hooker, the Fundamental Orders, King Philip's War, and the Charter Oak.

Link to this Internet site from http://www.myreportlinks.com

▶ Steam and Electric Locomotives of the New Haven Railroad
The New Haven Railroad Digital Collection Online presents a digital collection of steam and electric locomotives. You will also find a historical overview of the railroad, including the story of its conversion from steam to electricity.

Link to this Internet site from http://www.myreportlinks.com

Any comments? Contact us: **comments@myreportlinks.com**

Connecticut Facts

▶ **Capital**
Hartford

▶ **Population**
3,405,565*

▶ **Gained Statehood**
January 9, 1788, the fifth state

▶ **Motto**
"He Who Transplanted Still Sustains"

▶ **Nicknames**
Constitution State (official), Nutmeg State, Blue Law State, Brownstone State, Freestone State, Provisions State, Land of Steady Habits.

▶ **Song**
"Yankee Doodle"

▶ **Hero**
Nathan Hale

▶ **Heroine**
Prudence Crandall

▶ **Tree**
White oak (Charter oak)

▶ **Mineral**
Garnet

▶ **Bird**
American robin

▶ **Animal**
Sperm whale

▶ **Ship**
USS *Nautilus*

▶ **Folk Dance**
Square dance

▶ **Flower**
Mountain laurel

▶ **Shellfish**
Eastern oyster

▶ **Flag**
Five feet six inches in length and four feet four inches in width, the Connecticut state flag is made of azure blue silk. In the center is a shield with three supported grape vines bearing fruit. Under the shield is a banner with the words *Qui Transtulit Sustinet*, Latin for "He Who Transplanted Still Sustains," the state motto. The flag is bordered in gold.

*Population reflects the 2000 census.

Chapter 1
The State of Connecticut: Original Thinkers

Connecticut is one of the smallest of the fifty states. Only Rhode Island and Delaware cover less area. Despite its size, however, Connecticut is home to more than 3 million people, about the same as the combined populations of Alaska, Montana, North Dakota, South Dakota, and Wyoming. Ever since colonial days, the people of Connecticut have been coming up with unique, interesting ideas and inventions that have changed the way we live.

▶ Eli Whitney, Cotton, and Firearms

Until Yale graduate and New Haven resident Eli Whitney came along, the fiber in cotton plants was extracted from the seeds by hand, a very slow and expensive process. In 1793, Whitney invented a machine with spikes and a rotating brush that separated the fiber from the seeds by pulling the cotton fibers through slots. Whitney's invention, first called a saw gin and then a cotton gin, short for "engine," made it easier and less expensive to produce cotton. Soon thousands of acres in the South were covered by cotton plants, and thousands of slaves were needed to pick the cotton. Contrary to Whitney's intention, however, his invention led to an increase in slavery and thus helped to lead, indirectly, to the American Civil War, fought from 1861 to 1865.

Connecticut was also the home of another of Whitney's innovations—mass production through the use of interchangeable parts. Until 1798, firearms had been made one at a time, slowly and at great cost. In that

year in his arms factory in Whitneyville (part of the town of Hamden), Whitney was able to manufacture 10,000 muskets for American troops by producing parts that could be assembled at the same time and fit every firearm. It was one of the first mass-production facilities in the world.

▶ Eli Terry's Clocks

An East Windsor clockmaker named Eli Terry also employed the system of interchangeable parts in manufacturing clocks. By 1800 his factory in Plymouth was making twenty clocks at a time. By 1810, Terry's company made 4,000 identical clocks. Terry's company was also a pioneer in the use of brass parts in clocks, which made them stronger and more durable than clocks had been. Some of the clocks produced by Terry's factory are still running today.

▶ Colt and Goodyear

Until Samuel Colt invented a revolving cylinder that could hold several bullets, pistols could only fire once before reloading. By 1848, Colt's Patent Fire Arms Manufacturing Company was producing thousands of pistols at a huge plant in Hartford, his hometown. The Colt .45 became the most popular handgun in the world.

Charles Goodyear, an inventor born in New Haven, spent years trying to stabilize rubber so that temperature would not affect it. Nothing seemed to work until 1839, when Goodyear accidentally dropped one of his mixtures onto a stove and found that the mixture, which was sulfur combined with rubber, did not melt or burn. Instead it became a stable, useful material. Mixing natural rubber with sulfur, then heating it, was the answer. The process was called vulcanization. Soon Goodyear's method was used throughout the world.[1]

▶ McClintock, a Pioneer in Genetics

Early in the twentieth century, scientists knew that human traits and characteristics are carried on the tiny chromosomes found deep inside all living cells. But they did not understand how the chromosomes worked. Barbara McClintock, a geneticist from Hartford, helped explain the process. McClintock spent decades quietly

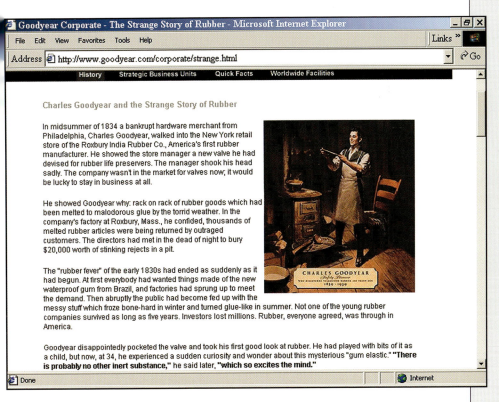

▲ Charles Goodyear, a native of New Haven, came up with a process in 1839 that allowed rubber to retain its shape regardless of temperature. Neither Goodyear nor his family was directly involved with the company that was named in his honor—the Goodyear Tire and Rubber Company.

studying the genes that made up the chromosomes of the maize, or corn, plant. Based on her studies and observations in the 1940s and 1950s, she was sure that genes jumped, or moved, between different chromosomes. Her research led to the discovery that certain genetic material changed its location on chromosomes from one generation to the next. Although her findings were not immediately hailed by other scientists, she was awarded the 1983 Nobel Prize in physiology or medicine.

▶ Edwin Land's Camera

Edwin Herbert Land, a physicist born in Bridgeport in 1909, invented polarized light filters, which eliminated glare from windows and photographic lenses. In 1937, he founded the Polaroid Corporation to make the filters.

Then in 1944 his young daughter asked him a question: She wondered why a photograph could not come right out of a camera, without having to wait for the film to be developed and printed. Land thought she posed an interesting question, so he went to work to develop such a camera. By 1948, his company was manufacturing the Polaroid Land camera, a revolutionary product because it produced complete black-and-white photographs in about a minute. Fifteen years later, his cameras could produce color photos.

▶ Connecticut Originals

Many of Connecticut's innovations have had important, long-lasting effects on the United States and the world.

In 1639, the colony's earliest settlers in the towns of Hartford, Windsor, and Wethersfield adopted the Fundamental Orders, the first written constitution that created a government in the Western Hemisphere.

Barbara McClintock did pioneer work in plant genetics. She received the Nobel Prize for Physiology or Medicine in 1983.

BARBARA MCCLINTOCK (1902-1992)

Barbara McClintock was born in Hartford, Connecticut. Her father was an army doctor and her mother was a piano teacher. McClintock was an active child and enjoyed many sports like volleyball, skating, and swimming. She had a passion for information, and in a time when a woman's career was a successful marriage, McClintock was determined to go to college. In 1918, she enrolled in Cornell University, the College of Agriculture.

Under the social and intellectual background of college, McClintock blossomed into a popular coed. By the time she finished her undergraduate credits, she found herself in graduate school in the new field of cytology. As a paid assistant in her second year of graduate work, she improved on a method that her employer was using and was able to identify maize chromosomes. It was a problem he had been working on for years and she effectively scooped her own boss.

When she finished her Ph.D. in 1927, McClintock knew that her next step was to map corn chromosomes in linkage groups like T. H. Morgan's group was doing for *Drosophila*. To do this work, McClintock stayed at Cornell as an instructor. She met fellow graduate students Marcus Rhoades and George Beadle who became lifetime friends as well as colleagues. McClintock helped Beadle sort out the *Neurospora* chromosomes. Beadle, with Edward Tatum, built on this work and developed the "one gene, one enzyme" theory using *Neurospora*.

Courtesy of Cold Spring Harbor Laboratory Archives. Noncommercial, educational use only.

▲ Born in Hartford in 1902, Barbara McClintock was determined to go to college at a time when many women were not encouraged to do so. Her pioneering work in plant genetics led to a Nobel Prize in 1983.

Other literary firsts include *The Hartford Courant*, first published in 1764 as the *Connecticut Courant*, America's oldest continuously published newspaper. And the United States had no dictionary of its own until Connecticut's Noah Webster published his first one in 1806. That dictionary is still being revised and used today.

The *Nautilus*, the world's first nuclear-powered submarine, was constructed and launched from Groton, Connecticut, in 1954. It was the first ship to travel under the ice of the North Pole.

Chapter 2

Land and Climate

Connecticut is the southernmost of the New England states. It is bordered by Massachusetts to the north, Long Island Sound to the south, Massachusetts and Rhode Island to the east, and New York to the west. The state's land area covers 4,845 square miles (12,550 square kilometers), making it the third-smallest state.[1]

Geographic Regions

There are five geographic regions in Connecticut: the Coastal Lowland, the Taconic Section, the Connecticut

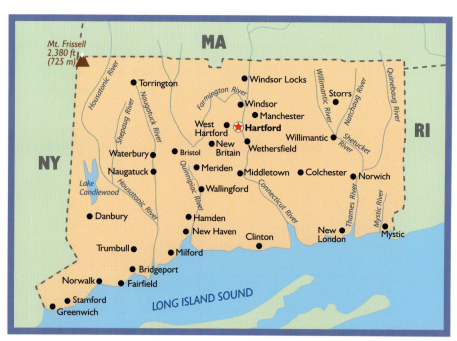

▲ A map of Connecticut.

Valley Lowland, the Eastern New England Upland, and the Western New England Upland. These regions actually extend beyond Connecticut's borders and are found in some of the other New England states.

The Coastal Lowland region in Connecticut is part of a larger region that hugs the New England coast. It is a thin strip of land, ranging from six to sixteen miles wide. This region features beaches and harbors on Long Island Sound, the body of water that separates the shores of Connecticut from Long Island, New York.

The Taconic Section of Connecticut is in the northwestern corner of the state. It contains the southern tip of the Taconic Mountains, which extend into New York. This region is home to Connecticut's highest point, Mount Frissell, which is 2,380 feet (725 meters) high.

The Connecticut Valley Lowland region runs through the center of Connecticut and extends north into Massachusetts. The Connecticut River, the state's largest and most important river and one that is deep enough to accommodate some small ocean-going ships, flows through the northern half of this region. The soil in this relatively low and flat region is quite fertile, providing good farmland.

The Eastern and Western New England Uplands on either side of the valley are slightly higher in elevation and contain less fertile soil for farming. The Western Upland is characterized by steep hills and many rivers (the Housatonic being the major river), while the Eastern Upland features lower hills but many forests. The Quinebaug and the Thames are the most important rivers in this region.

▶ Lakes and Forests

Connecticut is home to thirty state forests.[2] In fact, more than half of the land in Connecticut is covered with forests. They offer a friendly habitat for animals such as rabbits, squirrels, beavers, deer, and even some moose.

There are thousands of lakes in Connecticut, most of them small. They were carved out of the landscape thousands of years ago by glaciers. The largest natural lake is Bantam Lake, northwest of Waterbury. A dam on the Housatonic River formed Lake Candlewood, the state's largest lake, near the border with New York.

▲ Connecticut is home to ninety-three state parks and thirty state forests, offering residents and visitors the chance to enjoy hiking, skiing, boating, fishing, and bird-watching, among other forms of recreation.

The waters of Connecticut are rich with trout and other fish. Clams, oysters, and lobsters can be found in Long Island Sound.

▶ Climate

Connecticut has a temperate climate, especially when compared with the rest of New England. The summers are not too hot, and the winters are not too cold. The average temperature in January in Connecticut is 26°F. The average July temperature there is 71°F. The average annual rainfall in the state is 47 inches.

Severe storms and hurricanes are sometimes stopped from reaching the state's shores by Long Island, which acts as a barrier to the rough weather. But there were floods in 1854 and 1936, and in 1938, a powerful hurricane hit Connecticut and caused a great deal of damage.

▶ Connecticut's Cities

Bridgeport, with 139,529 people, is the largest city in Connecticut. Settled in 1639, Bridgeport grew up around the harbor where the Pequonnock River meets Long Island Sound. Bridgeport's first major industry was whaling. After railroads arrived in the 1800s, the city became an industrial center with many factories. Bridgeport was the childhood home of P. T. Barnum, the man whose circus, shows, and exhibits entertained the world. Today Bridgeport's Barnum Museum preserves his memory.

▶ New Haven, Home of Yale

New Haven, Connecticut's second-largest city with 123,626 people, was settled by Puritans who migrated south from the Massachusetts Bay Colony in 1638. New

▲ *A bird's-eye view of Hartford, the capital of Connecticut. The state capitol building is in the foreground.*

Haven is probably best known as the home of Yale University, one of the world's most prestigious learning institutions, which moved to the city in 1716. Many of the buildings on Yale's campus are beautiful ivy-covered colonial structures. Connecticut Hall, Nathan Hale's dormitory, was built in 1752 and is still in use. Yale also features extensive libraries and art museums.

▶ The State Capital

Hartford, Connecticut's capital and third-largest city, got its start as a Dutch trading post in 1633. Three years later, Thomas Hooker and Samuel Stone, the first English settlers there, renamed the settlement after Stone's hometown in England.

Today, Hartford, located in the center of the state, is a bustling city of 121,578. Since 1810 it has been the home base of many insurance companies. The Old State House, opened in 1797, is the oldest state capitol still standing. Now a historic site and a museum, the building literally opens and closes each day with a bang, when a cannon is fired. The current state capitol has been in use since 1878. Its dome sparkles with a gold-leaf covering.

▶ Stamford, Waterbury, and Mystic

Nathaniel Turner bought a parcel of land in the Connecticut Colony's southwestern corner in 1640. Over the centuries, the settlement on that land has grown into Stamford, a city with a population of 117,083. Because of its location and convenient railroad transportation, Stamford has become the home of thousands of people who work in nearby New York City. At the Stamford Museum and Nature Center, visitors can enjoy hiking trails and a planetarium.

Connecticut's original capitol, the Old State House, was completed in 1796 and opened a year later. Its architect, Charles Bulfinch, was also one of the architects for the United States Capitol.

Waterbury, situated on the Naugatuck River about halfway between Hartford and Bridgeport, was first settled around 1686. Its population is 107,271. For decades, the brass industry was Waterbury's most important industry, and the city is still known as the Brass City.

Mystic, on the southeastern coast of Connecticut, is a small village today, but 150 years ago, it was one of America's most important shipbuilding sites. The speedy clipper ships built in its shipyards traveled the world. At Mystic Seaport, founded in 1929 to preserve Mystic's maritime heritage, visitors can board replicas of the historic wooden ships that were part of the seaport's past.

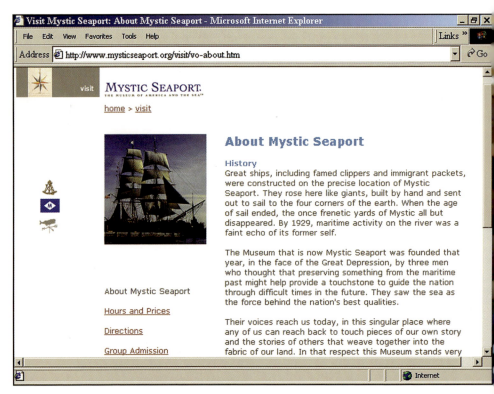

▲ The town of Mystic, Connecticut, is home to Mystic Seaport, the largest maritime museum in the United States.

Historic and Artistic Attractions

There are interesting places to visit in Connecticut beyond the state's cities. Hundreds of dinosaur footprints have been discovered near Rocky Hill, and many of them have been preserved inside a dome at Dinosaur State Park. Visitors are welcome to bring plaster to make their own casts of the prints.

The Mashantucket Pequot Museum and Research Center, in Mashantucket, focuses on New England history, especially the role played by the Pequot tribe.

Jonathan Trumbull was Connecticut's colonial governor during the American Revolution. He helped found the Sons of Liberty, a group of patriots, and served as an advisor to George Washington. Trumbull's home in Lebanon, once an important meeting place for patriots, can be visited today as a museum. Since 1910, the United States Coast Guard Academy has been located in New London. Cadets train there to become commissioned Coast Guard officers. Visitors can tour the academy.

Chapter 3
Famous Nutmeggers

Connecticut, the Nutmeg State, has been the birthplace or home of some of the most famous people in American history. One such Nutmegger was Nathan Hale, who gave his life for his country during the American Revolution and has been declared a Connecticut hero. Connecticut is the only one of the fifty states to have an official state hero and heroine.

▶ Revolutionary War Hero

Nathan Hale began his studies at Yale College in 1769 when he was only fourteen years old. After graduation, he became a schoolteacher in East Haddam and then New London. When the American Revolution erupted in 1775, however, Hale left teaching to become an officer in Connecticut's militia. The forts that Hale and his men guarded were never attacked, so Hale spent most of his time sorting out supplies and keeping records.

In the fall of 1776, Hale finally got a chance for some excitement. The British were preparing to attack from their camps on Long Island. General George Washington needed to know when and where they were planning to attack. Hale volunteered to go behind enemy lines to find out.

Hale crossed Long Island Sound and began wandering through the area, pretending to be a teacher looking for a job while secretly gathering information on British troop movements on the island and in New York City.

Unfortunately, he was captured by the British who found the notes he was carrying. When it became obvious

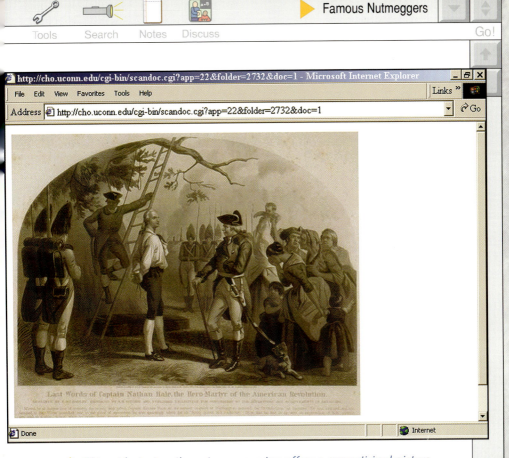

▲ This mid-nineteenth century engraving offers a romanticized picture of Nathan Hale's last moments. Hale was Connecticut's own "Hero-Martyr of the American Revolution," as the inscription below the painting reads.

that he was a spy, he was denied a trial and was hanged. Just before the noose was tightened around his neck, Hale uttered the words for which he has become famous: "I regret that I have but one life to lose for my country."[1] He gave that life at only twenty-one years of age.

▶ Thomas Hooker: Theologian, Scholar, and Colony's Founder

Thomas Hooker was a Congregational clergyman in England in the 1600s when his religious views, influenced

by Puritanism, brought him into conflict with the religious leaders of the time. Forced from his parish because of those views, he moved to the Netherlands, and in 1633 he joined other Puritan followers who had decided to make the long journey to the Massachusetts Bay Colony. Although Hooker became one of the religious leaders of that colony, he and some others grew dissatisfied and left.

In June 1636, Hooker and some one hundred followers settled in what is today Hartford. With groups from Massachusetts that had earlier settled in Windsor and Wethersfield, they formed the colony of Connecticut. By 1637, they had established the framework of a representative government. A year later, it became apparent that a more structured form of government was needed.

In a sermon he delivered on May 31, 1638, Thomas Hooker set the stage for that structure by asserting the rights of colonists to choose their public officials, to elect them by voting, and to limit the power of those in government. Hooker's sermon provided the direction that led in January 1639 to the colony's adoption of the Fundamental Orders, the first written constitution in the Western Hemisphere.

▶ John Brown, Ardent Abolitionist

In the mid-nineteenth century, most people in Connecticut were against slavery. It was such a terrible wrong that some of them felt that they should do whatever they could to stop it. John Brown stirred up passions on both sides of the issue.

Brown was born in Torrington in 1800. He had always been against slavery, but when he was in his fifties, he decided it was time to fight. In 1855, he followed his sons west to Kansas to aid in the struggle to make that territory one where slavery would not be allowed. A year earlier, the Kansas-Nebraska Act had given the settlers of new territories the right to decide on their own whether or not to allow slavery.

In 1856, Brown led a group that attacked settlers living on Pottawatomie Creek, where they killed five proslavery men. Many abolitionists applauded his violence and gave him money to buy supplies.

Brown then came up with a plan to free the slaves and set up a new state for them in western Virginia. In 1859, he and his men attacked the federal armory at Harpers Ferry, then in Virginia (today in West Virginia). They were defeated and captured. Less than two months later, Brown was convicted of treason and was hanged.

Another Connecticut native, abolitionist John Brown was called both a martyr and a madman, depending on one's views on slavery.

Many abolitionists considered John Brown a martyr, a fallen hero, while people in the South dependent upon slave labor saw him as dangerous and crazy. The quarrel over slavery grew louder and louder until 1861, when the first shots of the Civil War were fired.

▶ P. T. Barnum, Showman

Phineas Taylor Barnum, who was born in Bethel, Connecticut, and moved to Bridgeport, always wanted to be rich and famous.

Barnum moved to New York City in 1834, and a year later, he came up with an idea for making money and getting noticed. He came across Joice Heth, an elderly black woman who claimed to have been George Washington's childhood nurse. Barnum arranged for her to tour the country, telling stories about young Washington. Barnum claimed the woman was 161 years old, when she was only in her seventies or eighties. Of course, the whole story was ridiculous, but thousands of people bought tickets to see her, and Barnum finally became rich.

Over the years, he exhibited many very unusual attractions, including five-year-old Charles Stratton, a midget from Bridgeport, whom Barnum exhibited as "General Tom Thumb" from England. Barnum's exhibitions were popularly known as freak shows. The shows made P. T. Barnum rich and famous, and his fame also led to his being elected mayor of Bridgeport and to four terms in the Connecticut legislature.

Barnum went on to establish the modern circus with the man who had been his strongest competitor, James A. Bailey. Instead of producing a small show traveling in horse-drawn wagons, Barnum and Bailey staged a three-ring spectacle, lit by new electric lights and transported by

▲ Showman, promoter, and founder of Ringling Brothers and Barnum & Bailey Circus, billed as "the Greatest Show on Earth," Bethel, Connecticut, native Phineas Taylor Barnum was one of the most famous figures of nineteenth-century America.

special railroad trains. It was called "The Greatest Show on Earth." The Ringling Brothers and Barnum & Bailey Circus is still popular today.

▶ Dr. Spock

One of the most popular books ever written, based on the number of copies sold, is *The Common Sense Book of Baby and Child Care*. It was written by Dr. Benjamin Spock, a native of New Haven and a graduate of Yale University.

First published in 1946, the book revolutionized child-rearing practices in the United States. It has been translated into forty-two languages and has sold more than 50 million copies. Until the publication of Spock's book, most parents believed that it was best to be very strict and formal with their children. Spock's advice to parents was that it was more important to show love and tenderness to their kids and to actually enjoy them.

Not everybody agreed with Spock, however. Critics claimed that parents who followed his advice became too permissive with their children. But the book continued to sell. After retiring from his pediatric practice, Spock became active in politics. He campaigned against the Vietnam War and was even arrested for advising young men to stay out of the army. In 1972, he ran unsuccessfully for president of the United States.

▶ Political Pioneer

Money was in short supply in his family when Thirman L. Milner and his five brothers and one sister were growing up in Connecticut. Because of war-related injuries, his father spent long months in the hospital, and his mother cleaned houses to help support the family. To make ends meet, the Milners received welfare, or public-assistance money from the state.

Thirman Milner became one example of the welfare system working. In 1979, as a freshman state legislator, Milner spoke out in favor of an increase in welfare benefits at a hearing in the state capitol, saying, "I come as a product of the welfare system, not an exception, but from an average welfare family."[2] His point in that speech was that most of the people who received welfare benefits, as his family had, were not lazy or trying to cheat the system

▲ Thirman Milner served Connecticut as a state legislator and as the mayor of Hartford. He was the first African American to be elected mayor of a New England city.

in some way. As he said, "The myth of shiftless, do-nothing people living it up on welfare needs to die today."[3] With that speech, Milner helped to change the image that many people had of welfare recipients.

In 1981, Milner was elected mayor of Hartford, making him the first African-American mayor in New England. Milner served three terms as mayor and then was elected a state senator. Now retired from the state senate, he continues to counsel black political leaders and fight for the rights of those who are disadvantaged.

Chapter 4 ▶

Government and Economy

Hartford is the capital of Connecticut. Until 1875, it shared that distinction with New Haven. Now the center of state government is housed in the beautiful capitol building, which is topped by a gold dome

The state's government is divided into three branches. The governor, the head of the executive branch, is elected to a four-year term. Connecticut's citizens also vote for the state's lieutenant governor, secretary of state, treasurer, comptroller, and attorney general.

The legislative branch is the general assembly, made up of a 36-member senate and a 151-member house of representatives. Members of both houses are elected to two-year terms, and both conduct regular sessions during the first half of each year.

Connecticut's judicial branch is made up of four types of courts. The highest is the state supreme court with seven justices, each nominated by the governor and approved by the general assembly. There are also appellate, superior, and probate courts.

The state of Connecticut's representatives to the federal government are two U.S. senators and five U.S. representatives. In presidential elections, Connecticut casts seven electoral votes.

▶ ## Making Money

Connecticut is a relatively wealthy state. In 2001, its citizens had an average annual income of $41,930, the highest in the nation. Most Connecticut workers are employed by service industries. Those businesses account for about 75 percent of the gross state product.

▶ The Insurance State

The most important service industry in Connecticut is insurance. More than 50 insurance companies have their headquarters in Hartford, and there are 106 insurance companies statewide.[1] Connecticut has been the home of the insurance industry for more than 180 years. Marine insurance, which provided coverage for the ships and

▲ A Stonington fisherman mends one of his nets. Although the fishing industry in Connecticut is not as large as it once was, it is still an important part of the economy in Stonington, which has the only remaining commercial fishing fleet in the state.

33

cargoes that sailed from Connecticut's ocean and river ports to the Caribbean, had its beginnings in the state.[2]

Manufacturing, Agriculture, and Fishing

Manufacturing is responsible for about 20 percent of Connecticut's gross state product. The most important product is aircraft parts. Many cities have large factories that make components for jets and helicopters. Groton has facilities for making submarines. Some of the largest manufacturers of technology, including United Technologies, Xerox, and Union Carbide, are also based in the Nutmeg State.

While agriculture is not as prominent as it once was, farming is still important to the state's economy. There are about 4,000 farms in Connecticut. Dairy, poultry, forest, and nursery products are the most important products.

Connecticut's fishing industry is also much smaller today than it was when New London served as one of the main whaling ports in New England in the nineteenth century. Today, lobsters and oysters are the primary catches along with fish.

Connecticut's People

The population of Connecticut, according to the 2000 census, was 3,405,565—a lot of people in a relatively small area. Most of the state's inhabitants, or 81.6 percent, are white. The Hispanic or Latino population is 9.4 percent of the total population. African Americans make up 9.1 percent of the population, and American Indians make up less than 1 percent.

Chapter 5

History

Before European settlers arrived, there were only a few thousand American Indians in the land that would become Connecticut. They were all members of the Algonquian language group, but they were divided into several small tribes that often fought with each other. The biggest tribe was the Pequot, who lived in the southeastern part of the region.

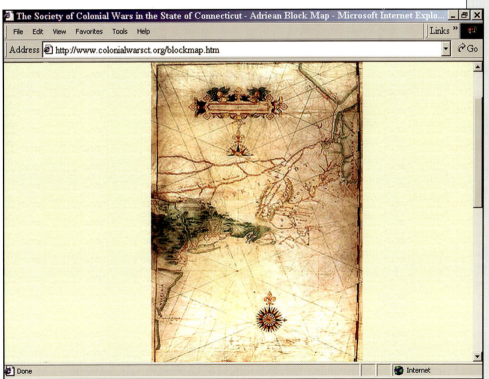

▲ The "Figurative Map of Captain Adriaen Block" was drawn following explorations from 1611 to 1614.

Besides the frequent wars, life for the tribes was good, since there was plenty of food: fish, corn, pumpkins, potatoes, and squash. Sometimes they even cooked popcorn.

An American Indian tribe gave the state its name: *Quinnehtukqut*, a Mohegan term that in English translates as "river place" or "beside the long tidal river." The term was adopted by the early white settlers to name the region and its biggest river.

▶ Early Explorers and Settlers

The first European to explore Connecticut was Adriaen Block from the Netherlands. He sailed his ship the *Restless* up the Connecticut River in 1614 and saw that the food and game that the Indians had was plentiful. He was especially impressed by the beavers and other wild, furry animals he saw.

Dutch fur traders who heard Block's stories poured into the new land and began to trade with the Pequot and other Indian tribes. The Europeans got beaver pelts; the Indians received rum and rifles. The Dutch started a settlement in 1633, built on the site of what is today the city of Hartford.

Soon they had company. That same year, John Oldham, an Englishman from the nearby Massachusetts Bay Colony, traveled south to explore Connecticut. And like Block before him, he was impressed by what he saw: plenty of food, lots of animals, and friendly Indians. Soon the English outnumbered the Dutch in Connecticut and eventually pushed them out.

▶ The Pequot Massacre

The Indians did not remain friendly for long, however, as the number of white settlers grew and began to take over more and more land. Some tribes, especially the Pequot, did not want to be pushed out as the Dutch had been. Soon the two sides were fighting. The English became infuriated after Oldham was killed in one of the attacks, and they decided to strike back. In 1637, Captain John Mason led an army of settlers and their Indian allies to the Pequot fort near Mystic. The plan was simple, according to Mason: "We must burn them."[1] His men set the fort on fire and killed anyone who tried to escape. Hundreds of Pequot died, most of them burned alive. The Pequot War gave the settlers ownership of the lands that the

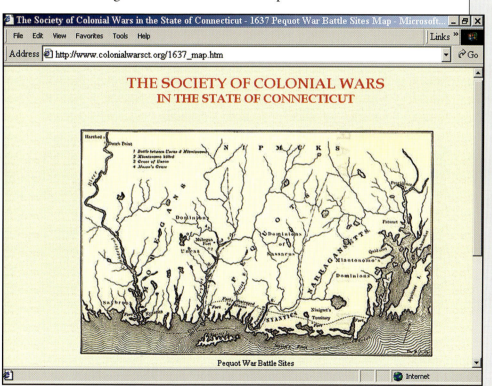

▲ This map shows tribal regions of Connecticut's American Indians at the time of the Pequot War, in 1637. Following the massacre of the Pequot at their fort near Mystic, the remaining members of the tribe fled, some going to Long Island, others to interior Connecticut, and a third group was captured near Fairfield.

Pequot had held as well as authority over the remaining tribes themselves.

The Fundamental Orders

A year earlier, Thomas Hooker, a Puritan and a Congregational minister who left the Massachusetts Bay Colony with a group of followers, settled in Hartford and, with some other colonists, established the colony of Connecticut. A separate group of Puritans established the colony of New Haven a year later.

Hooker was the driving force behind the Connecticut settlers who in 1639 drafted the Fundamental Orders, the first written constitution in the Western Hemisphere. In a sermon in May of the preceding year, Hooker preached that the men of the colony should be able to elect their own leaders and run their own affairs.

The New England Confederation

In 1643, a loose confederation was formed between the members of the New Haven, Connecticut, Massachusetts Bay, and Plymouth Colonies. Known as the New England Confederation, it was formed to provide defense for the new colonists in America.

In 1661, John Winthrop, Connecticut's colonial governor, traveled to London to secure a royal charter for the colony. Granted in 1662 by England's King Charles II, the charter established Connecticut's legal right to exist as a separate colony and guaranteed the male settlers' right to elect their own governor. The other American colonies at the time had governors appointed by the king. The terms of the charter also provided for the New Haven Colony to become part of the Connecticut Colony.

▶ The Charter Oak

Sir Edmund Andros, the appointed governor of several neighboring colonies, opposed Connecticut's freedom, however. In 1675, he sent troops to try to take over a fort in Saybrook. When he was convinced that the people of Connecticut would fight, he withdrew his soldiers. Twelve years later, Andros went to Hartford himself and demanded the surrender of the charter.

Colonial officials in Connecticut hid the document in a hollow oak tree. Andros never found it and returned home empty-handed. Connecticut had preserved its

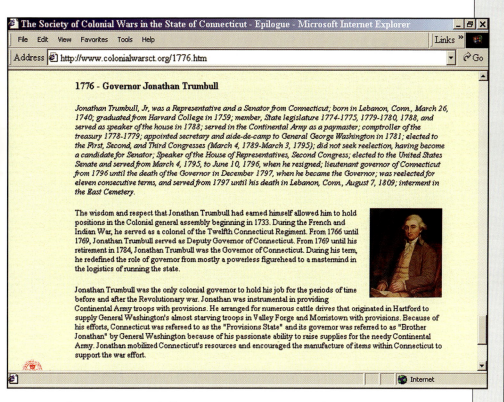

▲ Jonathan Trumbull was Connecticut's governor from 1769 until 1784. A native of Lebanon, he was the only colonial governor to remain in office through the American Revolution.

charter and kept its freedom, thanks to an oak tree that became known thereafter as the Charter oak.

The American Revolution

During the eighteenth century, the people of Connecticut became strong supporters of the American Revolution, which led to the United States of America becoming a separate, independent nation.

Jonathan Trumbull, from Lebanon, the colony's governor, helped organize the Sons of Liberty, a patriotic organization. Trumbull was the only colonial governor to remain in office after the war began, and he served in the Continental Army and was later appointed General Washington's aide-de-camp, a position of great trust. Hundreds of other Connecticut men joined George Washington's army. One of them, Nathan Hale, became a hero when he bravely faced death by hanging after being caught by British troops.

Connecticut is not nearly as proud of Benedict Arnold. He was one of the richest men in New Haven when he became an officer in Washington's army. He fought bravely and suffered severe injuries, but he did not feel that his work was appreciated. He decided to switch sides.

In 1781, Arnold led British troops on New London, which he captured and burned. Then at a battle near Groton, Arnold's men defeated an outnumbered American force. When the Americans attempted to surrender, Arnold's men killed most of them.

Despite Arnold's treachery, the Continental Army prevailed, and the fighting in the Revolutionary War came to an end in 1781 with a British surrender at Yorktown, Virginia. The new nation then needed to come up with a plan to govern itself, and Connecticut's delegates played an important part in the new country's constitutional convention in 1787. When the small states feared that the larger states would have too much power, the Nutmeggers came up with a solution known as the Connecticut Compromise. The House of Representatives in the new government would be based on population, but each state, no matter its size, would send two members to the Senate.

▶ Slavery, Civil Rights, and the State Heroine

In the late eighteenth and early nineteenth centuries, Connecticut's fertile land drew many to the state, and

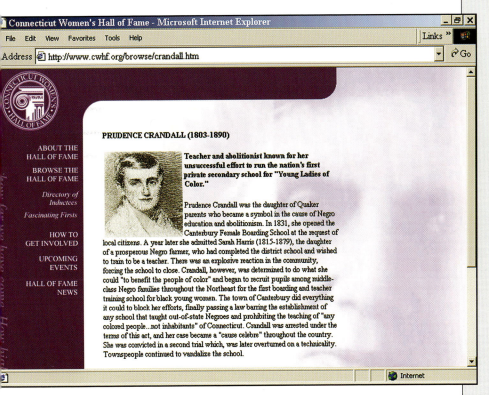

▲ Prudence Campbell, Connecticut's state heroine, was a teacher and an abolitionist who opened the first private secondary school in the United States for African-American women.

farmland became more scarce. As a result, people who wanted more land and new opportunities began to leave the state. Most of them headed west. They made their mark throughout the Union. In 1831, one fourth of the representatives and one third of the senators in Congress had been born in Connecticut.

Even though slavery had been abolished in Connecticut by 1848, the state played an important role in the events leading to the Civil War. Eli Whitney's cotton gin had created a need for thousands of additional slaves in the South. Harriet Beecher Stowe's novel *Uncle Tom's Cabin*, an antislavery novel written after the passage of the Fugitive Slave Act, helped stir up even more intense feelings about the "peculiar institution," as slavery was referred to in the South. Stowe was a native of Litchfield, Connecticut, located in the Northwest Hills.

The people of Connecticut might have hated slavery, but there was little support for giving free black men and women equal opportunity. When Prudence Crandall admitted a young African-American woman to her academy on the Canterbury Green in 1832, the parents of white girls withdrew their daughters. Crandall then decided to attract African-American women exclusively. In 1833, she established the first academy for African-American women in New England.[2]

The state of Connecticut, however, responded by passing a law that made it illegal for Crandall to run her school, and she was arrested and put through three trials, while her students were harassed for more than a year. On September 9, 1834, a mob attacked the academy and broke out its windows, and Crandall was forced to close her school. But her courage and desire to see young African-American women receive an education was finally recognized on October 1, 1995, when the state of Connecticut, by an act of the General Assembly, made Prudence Crandall the state heroine.[3]

Connecticut's Role in the Civil War

More than 55,000 Connecticut citizens fought for the Union in the Civil War. Twenty thousand of them were killed or wounded. The Union won the war, which lasted for four grueling years (from 1861 to 1865) and took more than half a million lives. The country was finally reunited, and with the ratification of the Thirteenth Amendment to

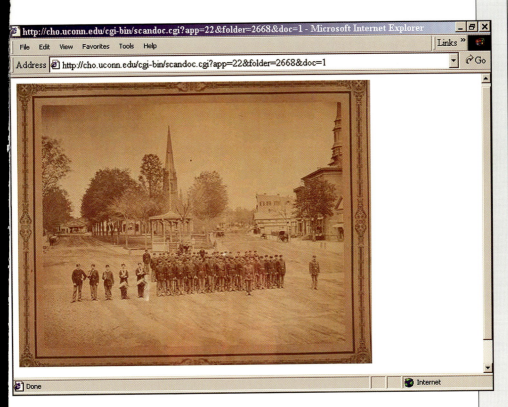

▲ This 1861 photograph taken in New Britain captures a muster, or assembling, of Civil War troops from Connecticut, probably from the regiment known as the Third Connecticut Volunteers.

the Constitution, in December 1865, slavery was finally abolished throughout the United States.

▶ Industry and Immigration

Until the mid-nineteenth century, farming was the most important economic activity in Connecticut. But during the 1800s and into the early 1900s, the development of railroads, mass production, and new factories made the state an industrial center.

The prospect of factory jobs encouraged thousands of European immigrants to move to Connecticut. By 1910, about 30 percent of Connecticut's residents had been born outside the United States. Almost 90 percent of the state's population lived in cities.

▶ The Twentieth Century: Depression, War, Recovery

During the Great Depression of the 1930s, millions of people across the country lost their jobs. Natural disasters made the situation even worse in Connecticut. A terrible flood on the Connecticut River wrecked large sections of Hartford in 1936. A hurricane two years later killed eighty-five people in Connecticut along the Atlantic Coast.

In the 1940s, during the years that the United States was involved in World War II, Connecticut prospered because its factories and workers were responsible for much of the munitions and other supplies needed for the nation's war effort.

▶ Postwar Years and Beyond

In the postwar years, the state's economy continued to thrive as old factories reopened and new ones were built. Like citizens in the rest of the country, thousands of

Connecticut's residents moved from the big cities to nearby smaller, newer towns, or suburbs.

Manufacturing declined in Connecticut in the latter part of the twentieth century. But the growth in the state's service industries—mainly in insurance, finance, and real estate—helped make Connecticut one of the wealthiest in the nation.

During this period, two interesting politicians from Connecticut brought the state into the national spotlight. In 1974, Ella Grasso, the child of Italian immigrant parents, was elected Connecticut's governor—the first woman to be elected the governor of a state on her own, without succeeding her husband or being appointed. And in 1981, Thirman Milner was elected the mayor of Hartford, becoming New England's first African-American mayor.

▲ The rural character of Connecticut is still evident in scenes like this one, a covered bridge in West Cornwall.

Chapter Notes

Chapter 1. The State of Connecticut: Original Thinkers
1. Colt's Manufacturing Company, Inc., *The History of Colt*, n.d., <http://www.colt.com/colt/html/i1a_historyofcolt.html> (February 12, 2003).

Chapter 2. Land and Climate
1. Borgna Brunner, *Time Almanac 2003* (Boston: Information Please Publishing, 2002), p. 144.

2. Ibid.

Chapter 3. Famous Nutmeggers
1. The Library of Congress, *America's Story From America's Library*, "The Revolutionary Period," n.d., <http://www.americaslibrary.gov/jb/revolut/jb_revolut_hale_1.html> (February 1, 2003).

2. Don Noel, Jr., *The Hartford Courant*, "Profiles in Connecticut Black History—Thirman L. Milner," n.d., <http://courant.ctnow.com/projects/bhistory/milner.htm> (December 12, 2002).

3. Ibid.

Chapter 4. Government and Economy
1. *State of Connecticut*, "About Connecticut," n.d., <http://www.state.ct.us/about.htm> (December 12, 2002).

2. Ibid.

Chapter 5. History
1. *The Colonial Gazette*, "The Pequot Massacre," n.d., <http://www.mayflowerfamilies.com/enquirer/native.htm> (December 11, 2002).

2. *The Connecticut Historical Commission*, "The Prudence Crandall Museum," n.d., <http://www.chc.state.ct.us/Crandall%20Museum.htm> (December 11, 2002).

3. *The State of Connecticut*, "The State Heroine," n.d., <www.state.ct.us/emblems/heroine.htm> (December 11, 2002).

Further Reading

Bailer, Darice. *Connecticut: The Constitution State.* Milwaukee: Gareth Stevens, Inc., 2002.

Burgan, Michael. *Connecticut.* Tarrytown, N.Y.: Benchmark Books, 2003.

Fradin, Dennis Brindell. *The Connecticut Colony.* Danbury, Conn.: Children's Press, 1990.

Gelletly, LeeAnne. *Harriet Beecher Stowe: Author of Uncle Tom's Cabin.* New York: Chelsea House Publishers, 2000.

Gelman, Amy. *Connecticut.* Minneapolis: Lerner Publishing Group, 2002.

Lough, Lori. *Nathan Hale.* New York: Chelsea House Publishers, 1999.

McNair, Sylvia. *Connecticut.* Danbury, Conn.: Children's Press, 1999.

Murphy, Jim. *A Young Patriot: The American Revolution As Experienced by One Boy.* New York: Houghton Mifflin Company, 1996.

Stein, R. Conrad. *John Brown's Raid on Harpers Ferry in American History.* Berkeley Heights, N.J.: Enslow Publishers, Inc., 1999.

Thompson, Kathleen. *Connecticut.* Austin, Tex.: Raintree Steck-Vaughn Publishers, 1996.

Index

B
Barnum, Phineas Taylor, 19, 28–29
Block, Adriaen, 36
Bridgeport, 19
Brown, John, 26

C
Charter oak, 40–41
climate, 19
Colt, Samuel, 12
Connecticut River, 17, 44
Crandall, Prudence, 42–43

E
economy, 32–34

F
Fundamental Orders, 26, 38

G
geography, 11, 16–23
Goodyear, Charles, 12–13
Grasso, Ella, 45
Groton, 15, 34

H
Hale, Nathan, 24–25, 40
Hartford, 12, 20–21, 26, 31, 32
history, 35–45
Hooker, Thomas, 20, 25, 38
Housatonic River, 17, 18

I
industry, 33–34

L
Land, Edwin Herbert, 14

M
Mason, John, 37
McClintock, Barbara, 13–14
Milner, Thirman, 30–31, 45
Mount Frissell, 17
Mystic, 22, 37

N
Naugatuck River, 22
New Haven, 11, 12, 19
New London, 23

O
Oldham, John, 36, 37

P
Pequot tribe, 23, 35, 37
population, 34
Puritans, 19, 26, 38

S
Spock, Benjamin, 29–30
Stamford, 21
state government, 32
Stone, Samuel, 20
Stowe, Harriet Beecher, 42

T
Taconic Mountains, 17
Terry, Eli, 12
Trumbull, Jonathan, 23, 40
Turner, Nathaniel, 21

W
Waterbury, 22
Wethersfield, 14, 26
Whitney, Eli, 11–12, 42
wildlife, 18
Windsor, 14, 26
Winthrop, John, 38

Y
Yale University, 11, 20, 29